BLACK BOX THEATRE PUBLISHING COMPANY

CATALOG OF PLAYS

ISBN: 978-1946613011

Printed in the United States of America.

ABOUT US

Black Box Theatre Publishing Company is an international publisher specializing in plays for school drama clubs as well as community and children's theatre groups worldwide.

Why are our shows so popular?

It's because they're fun, affordable and easy to stage!

We believe that theatre should be fun.

If it isn't then why bother?

We've made this catalog as easy to use as possible. Each page contains information on cast size, running time and royalty rates. If you are a drama teacher or a director and you find a play you would like to read, just contact us and we'll send you a copy to read and consider, absolutely free. We believe that if you read these plays, you'll want to produce them. We have something for everyone and we're publishing new work all the time.

All the information contained in this print catalog can also be found on www.blackboxtheatrepublishing.com.

TABLE OF CONTENTS

A MIDSUMMER NIGHT'S DREAM

Don't be afraid, it's only Shakespeare!!!

What happens when you mix two sets of star-crossed lovers, a group of blue-collar, would-be actors and a mischievous pair of feuding fairies in the woods one midsummer night? It's William Shakespeare's classic, four-hundred-year-old comedy, **A Midsummer Night's Dream**, come to life in this creative adaptation that all ages will understand and enjoy! This version has been formatted for younger actors and includes blocking suggestions and comedic business from previous productions!

Cast Size: 23 flexible roles with doubling possible.

Running Time: 90 minutes.

Royalty: $50.00 per performance.

Appropriate for all audiences.

A PERSECUTION STORY

Lydia, a born-again Christian, has lost her husband. Raising her only child, Agopolis, Lydia strives to teach him right from wrong. But, Marcus, a playful, playboy tax-collector, is always hounding her since losing his wife to an illness. Lydia resists Marcus, who reads every writing he can to try and figure out why his wife had to die. He doesn't believe in any God. That is, until his son becomes deathly ill. The Roman gods and doctors can't help, so he turns to Lydia's God, Jesus. After a miracle healing, Marcus puts his trust in Jesus. Then, the persecution starts. It has a happy ending, but the perils they go through are huge. A drama with comedic elements set around 325 AD.

Cast Size: 35 flexible roles with doubling possible.

Running Time: 90 minutes.

Royalty: $50.00 per performance.

Appropriate for mature audiences.

A SQUEAKY WHEEL GETS OILED

Everyone has heard the phrase, "it's the squeaky wheel that gets the oil" but how many people know the back-story? The story begins in a kingdom far, far away over the rainbow – a kingdom called Spokend. This kingdom of wheels is a happy one for the gods have blessed the tiny hamlet with plentiful sunshine, water and most important…oil. Until a terrible drought starts to dry up all the oil supplies. What is to be done? Without oil, Spare Wheel's squeak becomes so bad he loses his job and his family starts to suffer when his sick leave and unemployment benefits run out. What is he to do?

Cast Size: 10 flexible roles with doubling possible.

Running Time: 45 minutes.

Royalty: $50.00 per performance.

Appropriate for all audiences.

ABRAHAM LINCOLN: THE GREAT EMANCIPATOR

A short one act play about the 16th President of the United States that focuses on the humor, sentimentality and humanity of the icon.

Cast Size: 1M.

Running Time: 15 minutes.

Royalty: $50.00 per performance.

Appropriate for all audiences.

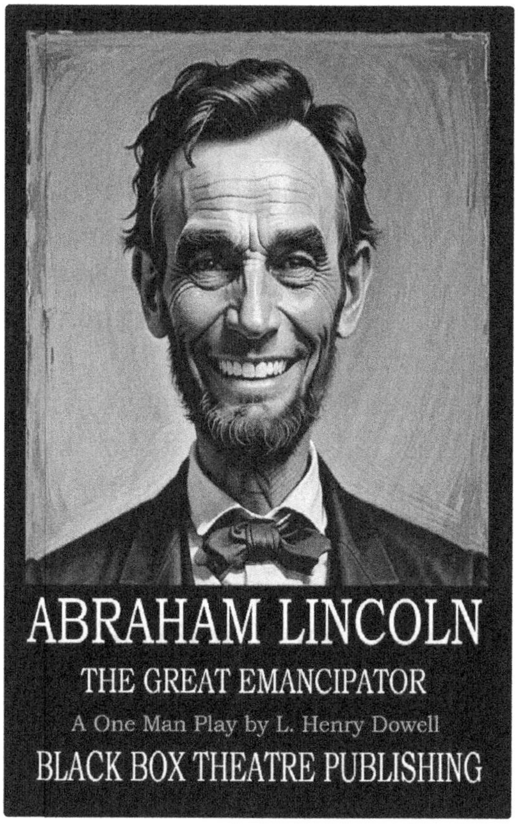

ADVENTURE PLAY COLLETION

A collection of several popular adventure plays together in one volume.

Hercules and Chuck
Jacklyn Sparrow and the Lady Pirates of the Caribbean
Jurassic Pork
Macbeth
Masked Men
Popeye
So, Who Was That Masked Guy Anyway?
The Long John Cafe
The Wacky Adventures of Robin Hood

For cast size, running time and royalty information, please see individual listings for each play in this catalog or on our website, www.blackboxtheatrepublishing.com.

BASED ON THE...

Four classic stories told in a unique form: a collection featuring duets and monodramas. Join two women, reunited schoolmates, examining the changes in their lives in "The Reunion" based on the classic poem "A Ruined Maid" by Thomas Hardy. Meet Kid Blink, union leader of one of the most successful and infamous strikes in history, in "Blink" based on the true story of the 1899 Newsboys Strike. "Lot 249" by Sir Arthur Conan Doyle inspired "The Mysterious Case of Lot 249"; a detective, on a mysterious killer's trail, doggedly interrogates a witness. And a young teenager tells the story of her unexpected pregnancy in "Miriam and Isa" based on the biblical story.

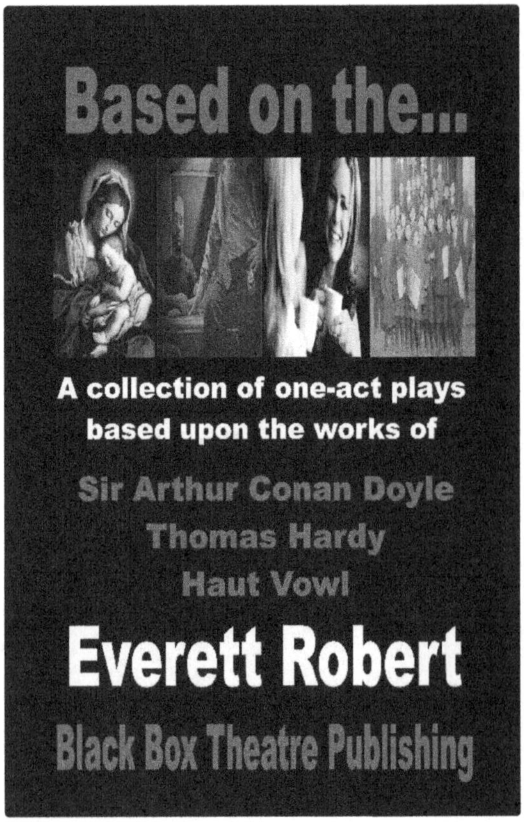

Cast Size: 2M, 2F, 1M, 1F (Each piece respectively.)

Running Time: Consists of 4 ten-minute pieces.

Royalty: $50.00 per performance.

Appropriate for all audiences.

BATGUY (FAMILY FRIENDLY VERSION)

"You ever mambo with Robert De Niro in a pale blue seersucker suit?"

Who is the mysterious Caped Crime Buster of Gothic City? Why, it's Batguy! The Dark Nut himself and he's on the trail of a criminal mastermind, a jerk named Jack! (Or is it the other way around?) Now you can introduce your audience to this hilarious, family friendly parody of the 1989 film starring Michael Keaton, Jack Nicholson and Kim Basinger!

Cast Size: 15+ flexible roles.

Running Time: 60 minutes.

Royalty: $50.00 per performance.

Appropriate for all audiences.

BATGUY (MATURE VERSION)

"It's been 25 years. Since that night. A homicidal clown. A rubber suit. Prince music playing in the background."

Your audiences will be rolling in the aisles with laughter at this Dark Nut! The Caped Crime Buster is here to save Gothic City from a real jerk...The Jerker!

Batguy is a hilarious, easy to stage parody of the 1989 Batman film directed by Tim Burton and starring Michael Keaton, Jack Nicholson and Kim Basinger.

Cast Size: 15+ flexible roles.

Running Time: 60 minutes.

Royalty: $50.00 per performance.

Appropriate for mature audiences only.

CINDERELLA AND THE QUEST FOR THE CRYSTAL PUMP

Cinderella and the Quest for the Crystal Pump, (Large Cast Version) is the story of a girl seeking a life beyond the chores heaped upon her by her grouchy stepmother and two stepsisters. Cinderella wants to go to the prince's masquerade ball, but there's one problem...she has nothing to wear! Luckily, her Fairy God-person has a few ideas. Meanwhile, Prince Charles Edward Tiberius Charming III, or "Charlie", has run away with his pals, Touchstone the Jester and the Magic Mirror, searching for a quiet place where he can enjoy a good book! Now this mismatched quartet find themselves on a quest to find the greatest treasure of all...the perfect pair of Crystal Pumps!

Cast Size: 29 flexible roles with doubling possible.

Running Time: 90 minutes.

Royalty: $50.00 per performance.

Appropriate for all audiences.

CINDERELLA AND THE QUEST FOR THE CRYSTAL PUMP

Cinderella and the Quest for the Crystal Pump, (Small Cast Version) is the story of a girl seeking a life beyond the chores heaped upon her by her grouchy stepmother and two stepsisters. Cinderella wants to go to the prince's masquerade ball, but there's one problem...she has nothing to wear! Luckily, her Fairy God-person has a few ideas. Meanwhile, Prince Charles Edward Tiberius Charming III, or "Charlie", has run away with his pals, Touchstone the Jester and the Magic Mirror, searching for a quiet place where he can enjoy a good book! Now this mismatched quartet find themselves on a quest to find the greatest treasure of all...the perfect pair of Crystal Pumps!

Cast Size: 13 flexible roles.

Running Time: 60 minutes.

Royalty: $50.00 per performance.

Appropriate for all audiences.

CROSSDRESSERS FROM OUTER SPACE

From the farthest reaches of the galaxy, the **Crossdressers from Outer Space** have come to Earth and boy, do they know how to accessorize!

Loosely based on Ed Wood's notoriously bad film, Plan 9 from Outer Space, this is a thoroughly ridiculous, absurdist, one-act play, perfect for college aged actors, directors, and audiences looking for something a little "different".

Cast Size: 5-10 flexible roles. (And 1 blow up doll.)

Running Time: 20 minutes.

Royalty: $35.00 per performance.

Appropriate for mature audiences.

CURIOUS TALES FOR CHRISTMAS

A collection of three Victorian Ghost Stories, **Curious Tales for Christmas** comprises of three pieces of ghostly horror.

Royalty: $35.00 individually, $50.00 together.

The Middle Toe of the Right Foot by Ambrose Bierce.

Cast Size: 1M.
Running Time: 15 minutes.

Playing with Fire by Sir Arthur Conan Doyle.

Cast Size: 3M, 1F.
Running Time: 20 minutes.

The Judge's House by Bram Stoker.

Cast Size: 3M, 1F with doubling possible.
Running Time: 45 minutes.

DEAR JOHN: AN ODE TO THE POTTY

"My dreams of thee flow softly,
They enter with tender rush.
The still soft sound which echoes,
When I lower the lid and flush."

They say that porcelain is the best antenna for creativity. At least that's what this cast of young people believe in **Dear John: An Ode to the Potty**! The action of this one-act play takes place almost entirely behind the doors of five bathroom stalls. This short comedy is dedicated to all those term papers, funny pages, and Charles Dickens novels that have been read behind closed (stall) doors! Bathroom humor at its finest!

Cast Size: 10 with 5M/5F roles.

Running Time: 15 minutes.

Royalty: $35.00 per performance.

Appropriate for high school and adult audiences.

DIVANALYSIS: THE MECHANICS OF CAMP

From the authors of Legends and Bridge and Seven Dreams of Falling, what came first the diva or the dress?

Divanalysis.

An informal lecture where the diva is deconstructed using Bette Midler, Liza Minnelli, Judy Garland and Karen Carpenter as examples. Parody meets fashion show in this high-concept drag fantasy from C. Stephen Foster and Carey Scott Wilkerson. A professor with too many ideas delivers a lecture on the metaphysics of the Diva only to have his spotlight dimmed when the very Divas from his analysis materialize to set the record straight...more or less.

Cast Size: Flexible. Can be performed with 2-5 actors.

Running Time: 90 minutes.

Royalty: $35.00 per performance.

Appropriate for mature audiences.

DORIS: THE WOMAN IN MISMATCHED BOOTS

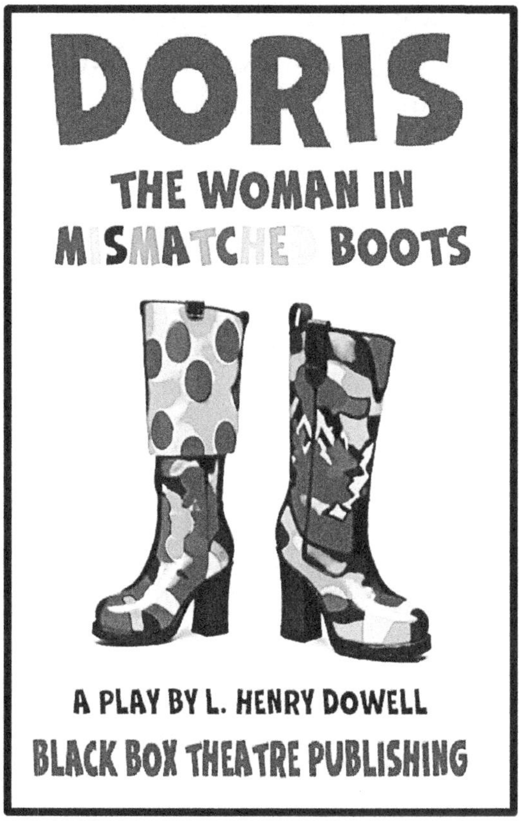

Meet Doris.

Her life was pretty routine until the morning she had to get dressed in the dark. Now everything in Doris' life seems upside down. Out of whack. Topsy Turvy. Things have changed. People who paid no attention before are starting to take notice of her. Some think she's a genius! Some think she's a lunatic! One thing is for certain. There's definitely something different about the woman in mismatched boots!

Cast Size: 15+ Flexible M/F roles.

Running Time: 30 minutes.

Royalty: $50.00 per performance.

Appropriate for all audiences.

DRACULA VS SANTA CLAUS

The battle of the century begins as two icons meet on stage for the first time in a battle for holiday supremacy! Gazillionaire department store mogul, B.G. Bucks, is up to his old tricks and he'll do anything to increase his stores' business and his bottom line. His plan? Create a massively profitable, super-duper shopping season by combining Halloween, Thanksgiving and Christmas into one big holiday... Hallowgivingmas! He'll manipulate Dracula and Santa Claus, the icons of Halloween and Christmas, into a knock-down-drag-out fight! It's the Count vs Kris Kringle! The Prince of Darkness vs Father Christmas! Nosferatu vs Pere Noel! It's Dracula vs Santa Claus!

Cast Size: 21 flexible roles with doubling possible.

Running Time: 70 minutes.

Royalty: $50.00 per performance.

Appropriate for all ages.

ELISHA AND THE BEARS

Based on the Old Testament story. The young people of Bethel learn what happens when you mock an old, bald man, and they will sure wish they had left him alone!

Cast Size: 15 flexible roles with doubling possible.

Running Time: 10 minutes.

Royalty Rate: $35.00 per performance.

Appropriate for all ages.

ELVIS MEETS NIXON: OPERATION WIGGLE

Declassified after 40 years!

On December 21, 1970, an impromptu meeting took place between the King of Rock and Roll and the Leader of the Free World.

Elvis Meets Nixon (Operation Wiggle) is a short comedy which offers one possible (and ultimately ridiculous) explanation of what happened during that meeting.

Cast Size: 2M roles with an offstage F voice.

Running Time: 10 minutes.

Royalty: $35.00 per performance.

Appropriate for high school, and adult audiences.

EVEN ADAM

In the beginning there was a man. Then there was a woman. And then there was this piece of fruit... ...and that's when everything went horribly wrong!

Even Adam is a short comedy exploring the relationship between men and women right from day one. Why doesn't she laugh at his jokes anymore? Why doesn't he bring her flowers like he used to? Who is that guy in the red suit? And just how did she convince him to eat that fruit anyway?

Cast Size: 3 with 2M/1F roles.

Running Time: 10 minutes.

Royalty: $35.00 per performance.

Appropriate for college and adult audiences.

EVEN MORE TWISTED

Did you know that Jack and Jill actually have a triplet named Jane?

Come along on this adventurous sequel to "Twisted Tales" where fairy tales get mixed up in a modern day twist. A stage manager is trying to navigate through teenage drama while weaving together three plays "Title", "Jack and Jill and Jane and Bill", and "Sleeping Bertha". "Even More Twisted" is wacky, hilarious, and will comically confuse the audience. This play can be produced without doing the prequel.

Cast Size: 15-40 flexible roles with doubling possible.

Running Time: 45 minutes.

Royalty: $50.00 per performance.

Recommended for all ages.

EXITS AND ENTRANCES

What would happen if a Noel Coward play intersected with a Marx Brothers film? You would get a farcical comedy set in the pre-World War II austere world where manners mattered, and a stiff upper lip ruled. Dickey returns to introduce his new bride Mable to his mum and dad. It turns out that Mable is the former mob moll for a NYC based Mafioso, Lou, who wants her back. He sends Sharky and Moose to bring back his girl. Havoc ensues, and the comedy goes from slapstick to absurd. The Father is a Nazi sympathizer, Mom is an overbearing social climber, Dicky is a rose color glasses fool for Mable until the maid steps in. See how it all resolves itself!

Cast Size: 11 roles with 7M/4F.

Running Time: 120 minutes.

Royalty: $50.00 per performance.

Appropriate for college and adult audiences.

FAIRY TALE PLAY COLLECTION

A Midsummer Night's Dream
Cast Size: 23 flexible roles with doubling possible.
Running Time: 120 minutes.

Peter Pan
Cast Size: 25 with doubling possible.
Running Time: 90 minutes.

Sleeping Beauty in the 25th Century
Cast Size: 13 with doubling possible.
Running Time: 45 minutes.

Winnie the Pooh
Cast Size: 17 with doubling possible.
Running Time: 75 minutes.

Royalty: $50.00 per performance.

Appropriate for all audiences.

FINGER LICKIN' GOOD! THE STORY OF COLONEL SANDERS

A one-man play about one of the most recognized faces in the world...Colonel Harland Sanders, founder of Kentucky Fried Chicken!!! Although he is most well-known for the eleven herbs and spices that made Kentucky Fried Chicken famous world-wide, Harland "Colonel" Sanders' life was about much more than fried chicken. The man whose face became synonymous with "finger-lickin' good" chicken used hard work and perseverance – not to mention a little luck along the way – to become recognized as Kentucky's most famous citizen.

Cast Size: 1M.

Running Time: 45 minutes.

Royalty: $50.00 per performance.

Appropriate for all audiences.

FOUR FAMOUS KENTUCKIANS

Abraham Lincoln
Cast Size: 1M.
Running Time: 15 minutes.

Colonel Harland Sanders
Cast Size: 1M.
Running Time: 45 minutes.

Jemima Boone
Cast Size: 1F.
Running Time: 30 minutes.

Dr. Ephraim McDowell
Cast Size: 1M.
Running Time: 35 minutes.

Royalty: $50.00 per performance.

Appropriate for all ages.

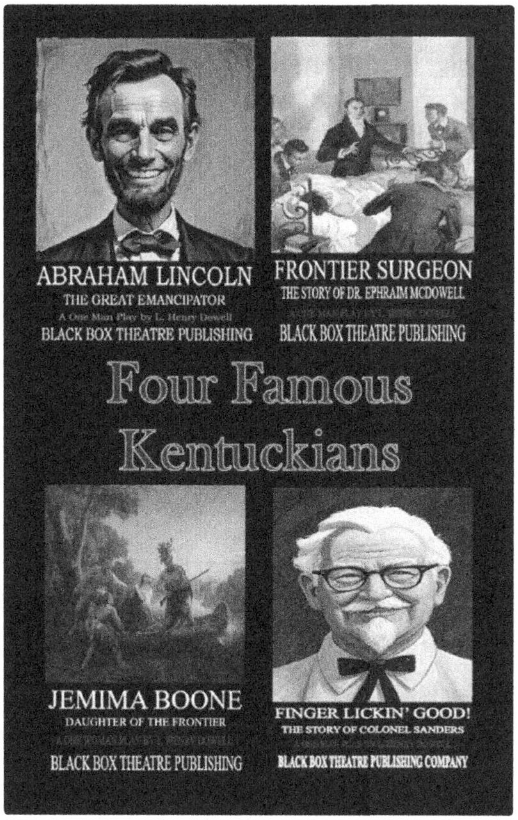

FRANKENSTEIN ROCKS!

It's monstrous fun for the whole family in this parody of the Mary Shelley classic! Dr. Victor "Vickie" Frankenstein has just inherited his grandfather's castle in foggy Transylvania but what secrets lie in the ultra-secret subterranean laboratory located beneath the castle?

It's a little bit monster story and a little bit Rock and Roll!

A perfect play for school groups and Community Theatres looking for something a little less scary and a whole lot of fun!

Cast Size: 16+ flexible roles.

Running Time: 60 minutes.

Royalty: $50.00 per performance.

Appropriate for all audiences.

FRANKENSTEIN'S MARY SHELLEY

A haunting tale of the creation of the groundbreaking book, Frankenstein as narrated by the monster himself. It's 1816, the Year Without a Summer and five friends are stuck indoors, bored, until one of them, Lord Byron himself, suggests a contest to see who can write the scariest story!

A mix of real-life events combined with a touch of the fantastic, this one-act play is perfect for groups looking for a competition piece.

Cast Size: 6 roles, 4M and 2F.

Running Time: 30 minutes.

Royalty: $50.00 per performance.

Appropriate for all ages.

FRONTIER SURGEON: THE STORY OF DR. EPHRAIM MCDOWELL

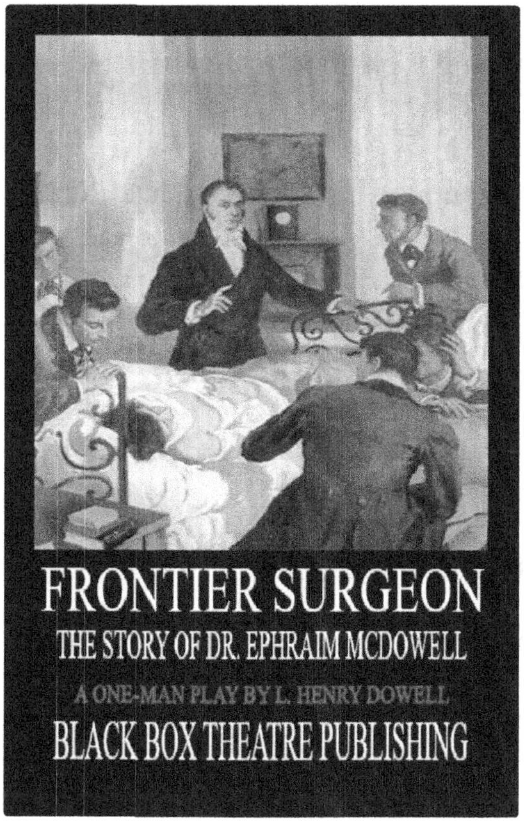

On Christmas Day 1809, a thousand miles from the nearest hospital and thirty-five years before the development of anesthesia, Dr. Ephraim McDowell removed a 22-pound ovarian tumor from the abdomen of a Kentucky woman.

It was the world's first ovariotomy, and it eventually brought McDowell worldwide acclaim as the Father of Abdominal Surgery.

Educational and inspiring!

Cast Size: 1M.

Running Time: 35 minutes.

Royalty: $50.00 per performance.

Appropriate for all audiences.

GODZILLA VS BAMBI

It's the showdown of the century as the King of Monsters takes on the Prince of the Forest in a winner-take-all-battle that your audiences will love!

Bambi had it all once. Fame. Fortune. You name it. But now they're calling him a "has been" and that doesn't sit too well with the hot-headed little stag. He's ready for a fight, so why not challenge the biggest, meanest monster of them all…Godzilla!

This isn't going to end well.

Cast Size: 14 flexible roles with doubling possible.

Running Time: 30 minutes.

Royalty: $35.00 per performance.

Appropriate for all ages.

HERCULES AND CHUCK

The legend of Hercules is known far and wide, but less is known about Hercules' younger brother, Chuckules or "Chuck" for short.

It's the biggest event at Olympus High, the Dodecathlon and the school's star athlete is ready to bring home the trophy until the unthinkable happens!

Now it's up to Chuck to save the day with his big brain!

Cast Size: 34+ flexible roles with doubling (tripling or even quadrupling possible!)

Running Time: 90 minutes.

Royalty: $50.00 per performance.

Appropriate for all ages.

HIGH SCHOOL LIVE

A play by Leslie Tanner, author of Jason and the Argonauts, Shorespeare, Night of the Muses and Middle School Live! **High School Live** is a series of skits that include parodies of high school life, outrageous news stories, rapping, a game show and so much more. Think Saturday Night Live for high schoolers!

This play needs a minimum of 25 characters but can be less if you are only using some of the skits.

Cast Size: 60 flexible roles with doubling possible.

Running Time: 60 minutes.

Royalty: $50.00 per performance.

Appropriate for all audiences.

HOLIDAY PLAY COLLECTION

A collection of popular holiday plays collected into one economical volume.

Dracula vs Santa Claus
Frankenstein Rocks!
Humbug! A Christmas Carol
The Dracula Spectacula
The Four Presidents
The Headless Horseman of Sleepy Hallow
The Pirate Who Saved Christmas
The Sleigh Team
Wanted: Santa Claus

For cast size, running time and royalty information, please see individual listings for each play in this catalog or on our website, www.blackboxtheatrepublishing.com.

HUMBUG! A CHRISTMAS CAROL

Humbug! is the story of Ebenezer Scrooge, a mean old man who hates everything and everybody! But of all the things he hates, he hates Christmas time the most! Then, one Christmas Eve, Mr. Scrooge is visited by some lively spirits who teach him the true meaning of Christmas.

It's Holiday fun for the whole family, in this easy to stage adaptation of the holiday classic!

Cast Size: 48 flexible roles with doubling possible.

Running Time: 120 minutes.

Royalty: $50.00 per performance.

Appropriate for all audiences.

HUMBUG! A CHRISTMAS CAROL (COMPETITION VERSION)

It's the award-winning competition version of one of our most produced plays!

Humbug! is the story of Ebenezer Scrooge, a mean old man who hates everything and everybody! But of all the things he hates, he hates Christmas time the most! Then, one Christmas Eve, Mr. Scrooge is visited by some lively spirits who teach him the true meaning of Christmas.

It's Holiday fun for the whole family, in this easy to stage adaptation of the holiday classic!

Cast Size: 36 flexible roles with doubling possible.

Running Time: 30 minutes.

Royalty: $50.00 per performance.

Appropriate for all audiences.

HUMBUG! A ONE MAN CHRISTMAS CAROL

A one man stage version based on the classic Christmas tale by Charles Dickens. This is the story of Ebeneezer Scrooge, a mean old man who hates everything and everybody. But of all the things he hates, he hates Christmas time the most! Then, one Christmas Eve, Mr. Scrooge is visited by some lively spirits who teach him the true meaning of Christmas.

It's holiday fun for the whole family!

Cast Size: 1M.

Running Time: 45 minutes.

Royalty: $50.00 per performance.

Appropriate for all audiences.

INFECTIOUS

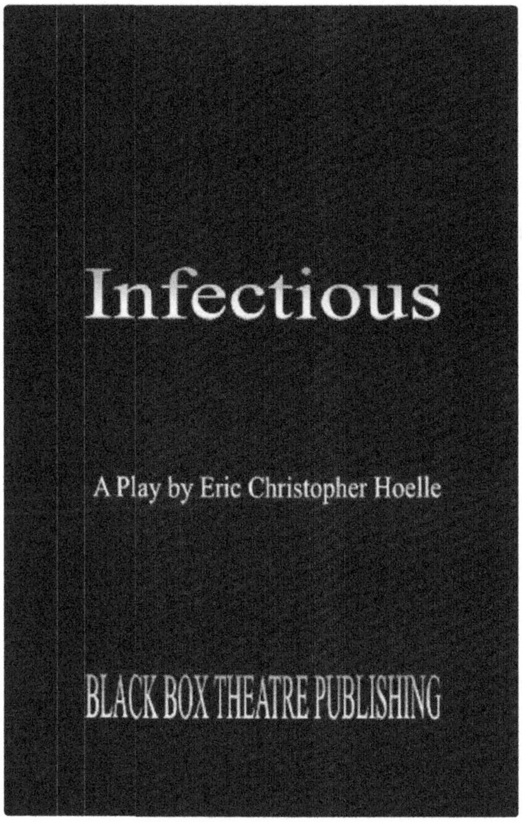

Infectious is an emotionally complex, physically startling drama that drags the darker elements of humanity to the foreground. In 1960, a strange and compelling man (Steve) from the North shakes up the monotony of a small Mississippi town when he stumbles across a grief-stricken, overwhelmed-by-life widow (Vivian). Just as Vivian learns the opportunities New York may have to offer, a crazed stranger shows up on her doorstep looking for Steve. Does corruption eventually take us all? Where is the line between responsibility and independence? How can you tell the difference between Love and Lust when your life is in shambles?

Cast Size: 5 roles with 3M/2F.

Running Time: 90 minutes.

Royalty: $50.00 per performance.

Appropriate for college and mature audiences.

JACKLYN SPARROW AND THE LADY PIRATES OF THE CARIBBEAN

Jacklyn Sparrow and the Lady Pirates of the Caribbean is a swashbuckling pirate parody with bloodthirsty buccaneers in massive sword clanking battle scenes! A giant wise cracking parrot named Polly! Crazy obsessions with eye liner! And who is Robert, the Dreaded Phylum Porifera? Of course, the whole thing ends with a large celebration where everybody gets down with their bad selves!

It's fun for the whole family!

Cast Size: 45 flexible roles with doubling possible.

Running Time: 120 minutes.

Royalty: $50.00 per performance.

Appropriate for all audiences.

JASON AND THE ARGONAUTS

Jason and the Argonauts is a fast-paced hilarious rendition of how Jason and his Argonauts captured the Golden Fleece. The large cast one-act comedy is filled with epic battles, dances, and a giant, fire breathing dragon. This play has many speaking parts as well as a large ensemble to accommodate a cast of any size. Perfect for schools, it also makes an outstanding competition piece.

Cast Size: 32+ roles with doubling possible.

Running Time: 40 minutes.

Royalty: $50.00 per performance.

Appropriate for all audiences.

JEMIMA BOONE: DAUGHTER OF THE FRONTIER

The daughter of Daniel Boone comes to life in this one-woman show capturing what life was like for a teenage girl in the early days of the frontier. On Sunday, July 14, 1776, Indians captured three teenage girls from Fort Boonesborough: Jemima, daughter of Daniel Boone, and Elizabeth and Frances, daughters of Colonel Richard Callaway. The Cherokee Hanging Maw led the Indians. The settlement was thrown into a turmoil and a rescue party was organized by Boone. The girls attempted to mark their trail. The third morning, as the Indians were building a fire for breakfast, the rescuers came up. The Indians retreated, leaving the girls to be escorted home.

Cast Size: 1F.

Running Time: 40 minutes.

Royalty: $50.00 per performance.

Appropriate for all audiences.

JURASSIC PORK

The Three Little Pigs meet Jurassic Park in this comic mash up for all ages by L. Henry Dowell.

Eager to escape the clutches of the Big, Bad Wolf once and for all, the Three Little Pigs build a time machine and travel back 150 million years to the Jurassic era where they quickly discover they have problems bigger than the Big Bad Wolf. Much, much, much bigger!!!

Cast Size: 6+ flexible roles with extras possible.

Running Time: 45 minutes.

Royalty: $35.00 per performance.

Appropriate for all audiences.

LADY PIRATES OF THE CARIBBEAN

Why should the boys get to have all the fun? **Lady Pirates of the Caribbean** is a swashbuckling pirate parody with bloodthirsty buccaneers in massive sword clanking battle scenes! A giant wise cracking parrot named Polly! Crazy obsessions with eye liner! And just who is Robert, the Dreaded Phylum Porifera?

It's fun for the whole family in this lampoon of everything you love about pirates! AAAARRRRRG!!!

Cast Size: 13 roles with doubling possible.

Running Time: 45 minutes.

Royalty: $50.00 per performance.

Appropriate for all audiences.

LADY PIRATES OF THE CARIBBEAN (COMPETITION VERSION)

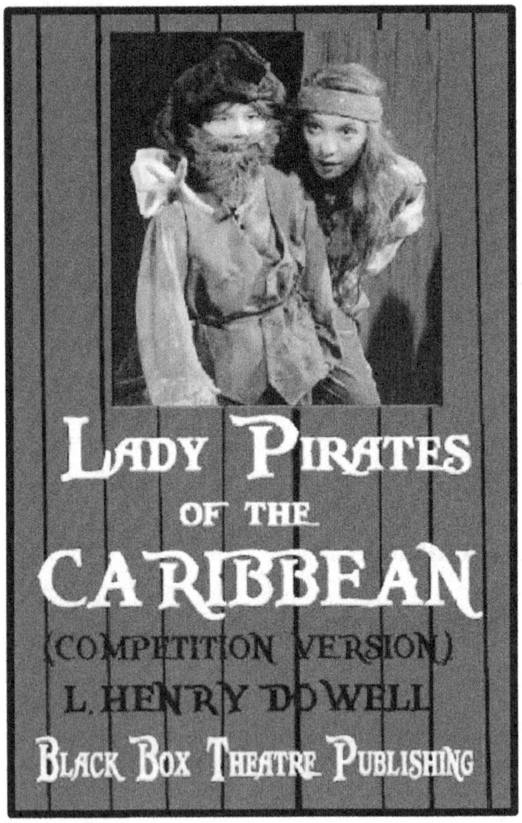

Is your school looking for an exciting new play for competition? Black Box Theatre Publishing presents a competition version of one of our most beloved plays!

Lady Pirates of the Caribbean (Competition Version) is a swashbuckling pirate parody with bloodthirsty buccaneers in massive sword clanking battle scenes! A giant wise cracking parrot named Polly! Crazy obsessions with eye liner! And who is Robert, the Dreaded Phylum Porifera? It's fun for the whole family in this lampoon of everything you love about pirates! AAAARRRRRG!!!

Cast Size: 26+ flexible roles with doubling possible.

Running Time: 30 minutes.

Royalty: $50.00 per performance.

Appropriate for all audiences.

LEGENDS AND BRIDGE

Legends and Bridge is a comedy imagining former, silver-screen legend Joan Crawford, who invites Judy Garland and Bette Davis up to her Manhattan apartment in 1964 to live with her as they work on a "secret" film project. After much prodding from Bette and Judy, Joan reveals the project she has in mind is a screen adaptation of "St. Joan" with Judy and Bette playing bit characters while she stars as St. Joan. After hearing this denture-shattering news, all hell breaks loose as each legend tries to maintain her position as top diva. Throw in a young boy toy that Bette brings home and a drunk Tennessee Williams and watch the comedy unfold.

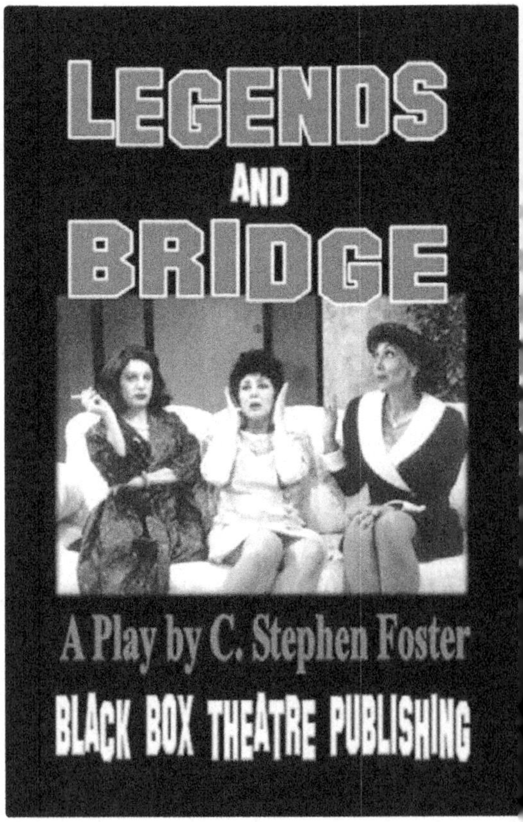

Cast Size: 6 flexible roles.

Running Time: 120 minutes.

Royalty: $50.00 per performance.

Appropriate for adult audiences.

LESSONS IN LEVITATION

Transformation, transcendence, escape, and even plain old flight - all recurring themes in Carey Scott Wilkerson's writing for the page and stage. Whether he is exploring the untold backstory of the Icarus myth or the campy-mystical life of a rural-Georgia folk artist, Wilkerson "searches for the human drama in legendary tales and the hidden magic in everyday life." Here, together for the first time, are the librettos of the two operas that have their feet on the ground but offer us lessons in levitation.

Cast Size for Eddie Stone: 8 roles for 1 performer.
Cast Size for The Ariadne Songs: 4-7 roles.

Running Time for Eddie Stone: 60 minutes.
Running Time for The Ariadne Songs: 60 minutes.

Royalty Rate: $60.00 per performance.

Appropriate for adult audiences.

LOSERS

An old timey Vaudeville type routine perfect for college-aged actors. Sebastian and Mortimer are a couple of college students, "losers" by their own estimation and the world at large, according to them. They have no car, no money, and subsequently, no girlfriends either, and for the low, low, price of $19.95, they'll show you how to be a "loser", too! Humorous and poignant, this show will have you thinking deep while you are rolling in the aisles!

Cast Size: 2M.

Running Time: 30 minutes.

Royalty Rate: $35.00 per performance.

Appropriate for mature audiences only.

MACBETH

"There can be only one King!"

In a not so distant future, the worst thing imaginable has happened. The great cities of the world lay in ruin. The few souls who survive wander as nomads swearing allegiance to various warlords. The greatest of these being Duncan, of Scotland. Now, in a post-apocalyptic fortress, one man plots his ascension. But what is Macbeth's destiny? Greatness...or Death?

Cast Size: 17+ flexible roles.

Running Time: 90 minutes.

Royalty: $50.00 per performance.

Appropriate for high school and adult audiences.

MASKED MEN

Towards the end of their illustrious careers, two famous masked men of the old west find themselves on the trail of the same outlaw gang. While sitting around the campfire these old friends discuss important concepts such as truth, justice, stubborn horses, masks, the expense of silver bullets and what actually constitutes "good jerky".

Cast Size: 2M.

Running Time: 30 minutes.

Royalty: $50.00 per performance.

Appropriate for high school and adult audiences.

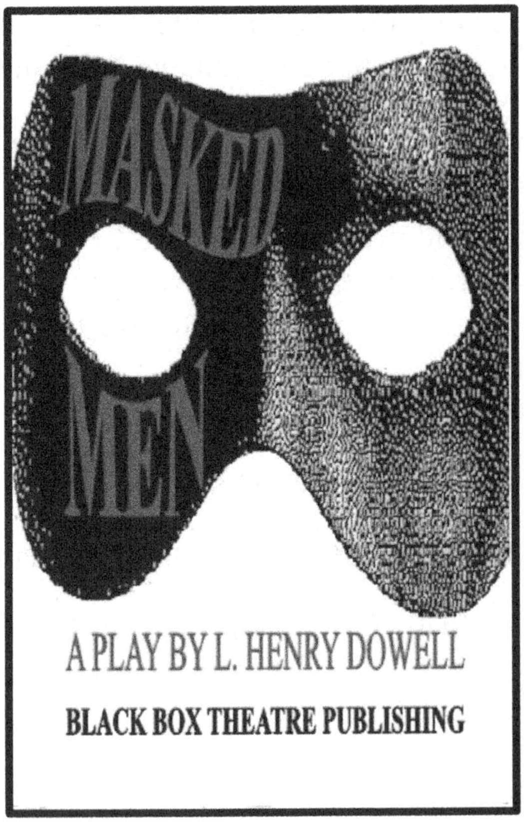

MIDDLE SCHOOL LIVE

Middle School Live was collaboratively written with the 8th grader drama class and teacher, Leslie Tanner, at Henley Middle School in Charlottesville, Virginia. "Middle School Live" is a series of skits that include parodies of middle school life, outrageous news stories, fairy tale characters rapping, a game show and so much more. Each skit is weaved together by Seussical commercials filled with songs and dancing. Think Saturday Night Live, but middle school style.

This play needs a minimum of 25 characters but can be less if you are only using some of the skits.

Cast Size: 60 flexible roles with doubling possible.

Running Time: 60 minutes.

Royalty: $50.00 per performance.

Appropriate for all audiences.

MISS HICKEY'S HICKEY

Teachers are people too...aren't they?

That's the question at the heart of this one-act absurdist play by L. Henry Dowell. When Miss Hickey shows up for class with a hickey on her neck, everyone is concerned about what it means. The students. The parents. The principal. The newspaper. Even the teachers' union rep! It's a hilarious look at something teachers face every day.

Cast Size: 9 flexible roles.

Running Time: 20-30 minutes.

Royalty: $35.00 per performance.

Appropriate for middle school, high school and adult audiences.

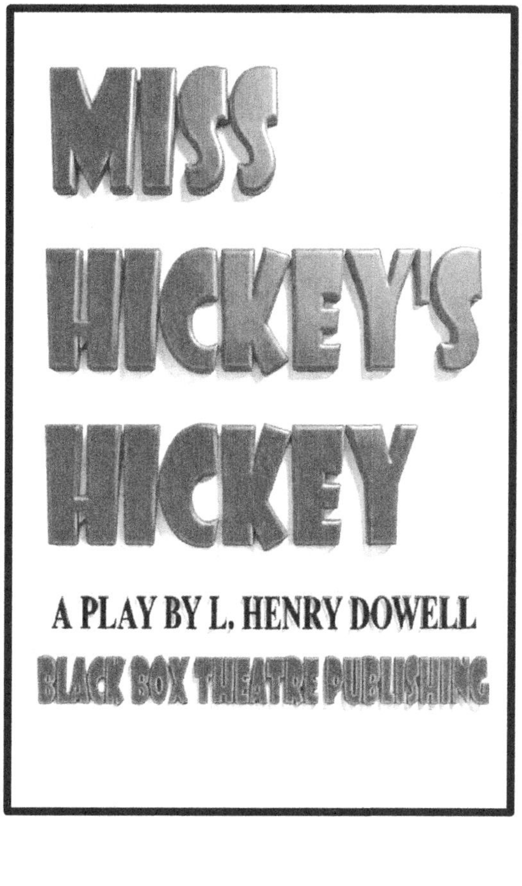

MY FATHER AND SON

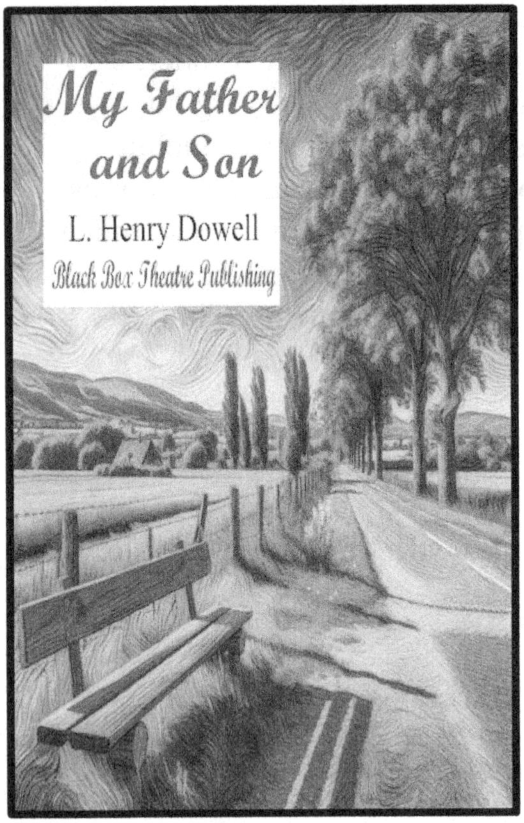

A one-act play by L. Henry Dowell.

Two strangers meet along the path between Heaven and Earth, where they stop to have a seat on a bench and strike up a conversation, soon realizing they have something very important in common.

Inspired, in part, by the song "The Living Years" by Mike and the Mechanics.

Cast Size: 2M.

Running Time: 10 minutes.

Royalty: $35.00 per performance.

Appropriate for all ages.

NIGHT OF THE MUSES

A modern family gets swept into the dreams of their teenage girl, Julia. She's a typical teenage girl feeling overwhelmed by her life: new girl in town, boyfriend troubles, annoying parents, school stress, and just feeling ugly and socially awkward. When she falls asleep after an evening of teenage troubles, Morpheus appears to shape her dreams. He summons the Muses to weave Julia's dreams, and upon her awakening, Julia finds inspiration to face her teenage troubles.

Cast Size: 30+ flexible roles with doubling possible.

Running Time: 40 minutes.

Royalty: $50.00 per performance.

Appropriate for all audiences.

PETER PAN

An easy to stage adaptation of the classic play by J. M. Barrie.

Peter Pan is a boy who never grew up. One magical night, he takes the children, Wendy, John, and Michael Darling to his home in Neverland, where Wendy becomes a mother like figure to all of the Lost Boys. The children go on adventures with fairies, mermaids, and pirates...including the over the top Captain Hook!

Cast Size: 25 flexible roles with doubling possible.

Running Time: 90 minutes.

Royalty: $50.00 per performance.

Appropriate for all ages.

PETER PAN (COMPETITION VERSION)

It's an easy to stage, competition version of Peter Pan by L. Henry Dowell, based on the original works of J. M. Barrie.

The play begins in the Darling household, where Wendy, John, and Michael are surprised by the arrival of Peter Pan and Tinker Bell. Peter came to retrieve his shadow and revealed that he lives in Neverland as captain of the Lost Boys. Wendy and her brothers fly with Peter to Neverland, populated by mermaids and villainous pirates led by Captain Hook and a crocodile who wishes to eat the rest of him. At last, the children return to London, leaving Peter Pan to his perpetual boyhood.

Cast Size: 22+ flexible roles with doubling or expanding possible.

Running Time: 30 minutes.

Royalty: $50.00 per performance.

Appropriate for all ages.

PLAN 9 FROM OUTER SPACE

This wacky one-act spoof is loosely based on the Ed Wood movie, widely considered to be the worst movie ever made!

It's a great fit for college actors and audiences of anyone else who loves the bizarre! Remember, it's perfectly acceptable to cut corners when staging this production.

As Ed Wood would have said, "It's not about the little details. It's about the big picture!"

Cast Size: 5-10 flexible roles.

Running Time: 20 minutes.

Royalty: $35.00 per performance.

Appropriate for mature audiences.

POPEYE THE SAILOR MAN

He's strong to the finich cause he eats his spinach...and that's a good thing because he's going to need all the strength he can muster to find the great white whale, Moby Dick! (With apologies to Herman Melville.)

Cast Size: 20 flexible roles with doubling possible.

Running Time: 30 minutes.

Royalty Rate: $50.00 per performance.

Appropriate for all ages.

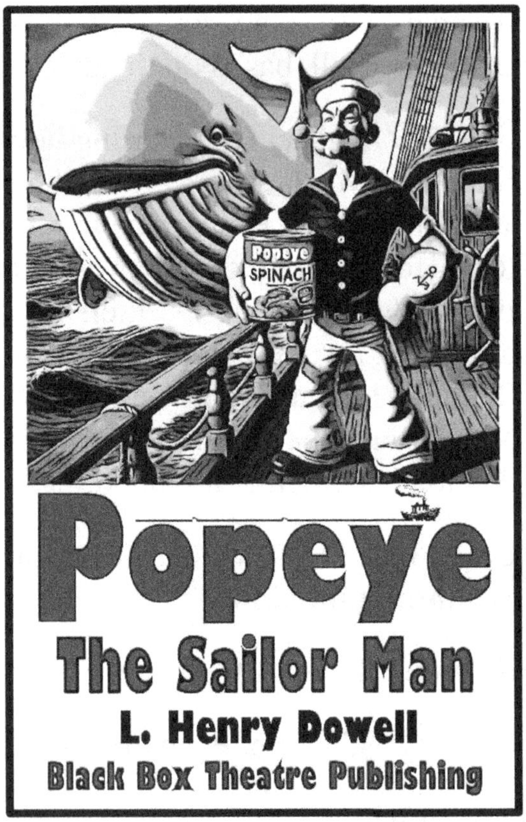

PULLING LEATHER (FAMILY FRIENDLY VERSION)

The term ‘pulling leather’ is used when a bronc rider touches any part of the saddle or the horse with their free hand during the eight-second ride, disqualifying them. Jacob Thomas has been riding since he was a little boy and is very good at what he does. But lately, he’s lost his confidence and he needs to get it back. He’s got scouts watching him. Throughout his struggle to regain his confidence, Jacob learns of a dark secret from his past, and finds true love that comes with a price. Will Jacob be able to get his confidence back, or will those two events cause him to give up what he truly loves, the rodeo?

Cast Size: 8 flexible roles.

Running Time: 120 minutes.

Royalty: $50.00 per performance.

Appropriate for all audiences.

PULLING LEATHER (MATURE VERSION)

The term ‘pulling leather’ is used when a bronc rider touches any part of the saddle or the horse with their free hand during the eight-second ride, disqualifying them. Jacob Thomas has been riding since he was a little boy and is very good at what he does. But lately, he’s lost his confidence and he needs to get it back. He’s got scouts watching him. Throughout his struggle to regain his confidence, Jacob learns of a dark secret from his past, and finds true love that comes with a price. Will Jacob be able to get his confidence back, or will those two events cause him to give up what he truly loves, the rodeo?

Cast Size: 8 flexible roles.

Running Time: 120 minutes.

Royalty: $50.00 per performance.

Appropriate for adult audiences.

PURSUED BY A RUNAWAY TRAIN

To save his parents' marriage, Jake searches for a legal way to make a lot of money quickly to cover his father's gambling debts. He decides to train hop and convinces his friend, Billy, to join him in his plan to catch a serial killer who murders hobos and collect the reward. Tragedy befalls Billy on the rails, and even after 40 years, guilt still burns through Jake's heart.

Will Jake ever find peace? Find out in this thrilling drama.

Cast Size: 15, 9M, 4F, 2 flexible with doubling possible.

Running Time: 75 minutes.

Royalty Rate: $50.00 per performance.

Appropriate for mature audiences.

RAPUNZEL: ESCAPE FROM ZOMBIE TOWER

Continuing our successful line of mash-ups, it's equal parts fairy tale and zombie apocalypse as Rapunzel the long-haired princess from the tower joins forces with a group of zombie hunters including Constable Grimey, his son Coral, a female samurai, a thief, a crossbow toting archer and a red headed giant to rid the kingdom of a horde of the walking deceased!

It's fun for the whole family!

Cast Size: 20+ flexible roles.

Running Time: 45 minutes.

Royalty: $50.00 per performance.

Appropriate for all audiences.

ROSES ARE RED: A 1930'S RADIO DRAMA

In this radio drama by S. Christopher Boggs, Adolf Hitler has ordered his soldiers to scour the globe for rare artifacts, paintings, etc. One such artifact, the lost shield of Sir Lancelot of the Lake, is discovered in the swamps of South Whales. To keep Hitler from obtaining the shield, archeologists ship it to America for safe keeping. College student Patricia Kelly and her fiancé, Ross Murdoc, are thrust into a game of cat and mouse at a dinner party. The other dinner guests begin dropping like flies, victims of a fiendish murderer. Who's the killer? Could the shield be the cause? Designed as a radio show script, "Roses are Red", can be produced in front of a live "studio" audience, or it can be recorded for radio/podcast rebroadcast.

Cast Size: 12 roles with 9M/3F.

Running Time: 120 minutes.

Royalty: $50.00 per performance.

Appropriate for all audiences.

SECOND YEAR ITCH

Chet and Brian find themselves suffering from a dry spell in their relatively new relationship. To spice things up, they decide to ask a third party to participate in their sex lives, someone they meet online. Enter Jaimie, a sweet but not too bright homeless "trick" who after a night with the couple, decides not to leave the next morning. Their relationship with Jaimie moves from a one-night stand to that of a son which makes Chet and Brian realize their emotional commitment and responsibility to each other. Suddenly, a promiscuous houseguest threatens their new family.

Cast Size: 4 flexible roles.

Running Time: 60 minutes.

Royalty: $35.00 per performance.

Appropriate for adult audiences.

SEVEN DREAMS OF FALLING

Seven Dreams of Falling is a post-modern re-thinking of the Icarus myth. It's late in the day and Icarus has grown weary of falling out of the sky: in painting, poetry, and myth. Having decided it's time for a career change, he plots his escape from a cycle of doomed repetition. Can Icarus simply fly out of his own life? And if he can, what does that mean for those he leaves behind: Deadalus, a father for whom rules, rituals and quantum mechanics are sacred; Theseus, a fading hero who loves the monster he must kill; Ariadne, the hero's former flame, the monster's half-sister, Lesbian cultural-critic; and the monster himself, The Minotaur, who holds a secret that could destroy them all...or set them free.

Cast Size: 5 flexible roles.

Running Time: 60 minutes.

Royalty: $50.00 per performance.

Appropriate for adult audiences.

SHORESPEARE (LARGE CAST VERSION)

Shorespeare is loosely based on A Midsummer Night's Dream. Shakespeare, with the help of Cupid, has landed at the Jersey Shore. Cupid inspires him to write a play about two sweethearts, Cleo and Toni. Shakespeare is put off by them but decides to send the two teenagers on a course of true love. Toni and Cleo are determined to get married right after they graduate from high school, but they must pass this course of true love that Cupid's pixies create. After these lessons, the sweethearts decide that marriage should wait, and Cupid is proud of Shakespeare who has finally reached out to the modern youth.

Cast Size: 26 flexible speaking roles with extras. Doubling possible.

Running Time: 90 minutes.

Royalty: $50.00 per performance.

Appropriate for all audiences.

SHORESPEARE (SMALL CAST VERSION)

Shorespeare is loosely based on A Midsummer Night's Dream. Shakespeare, with the help of Cupid, has landed at the Jersey Shore. Cupid inspires him to write a play about two sweethearts, Cleo and Toni. Shakespeare is put off by them, but decides to send the two teenagers on a course of true love. Toni and Cleo are determined to get married right after they graduate from high school, but they must pass this course of true love that Cupid's pixies create. After these lessons, the sweethearts decide that marriage should wait, and Cupid is proud of Shakespeare who has finally reached out to the modern youth.

Cast Size: 15 flexible speaking roles with extras. Doubling possible.

Running Time: 60 minutes.

Royalty: $50.00 per performance.

Appropriate for all audiences.

SLEEPING BEAUTY IN THE 25th CENTURY

Once upon a time, a beautiful princess was placed under a magic spell by an evil fairy. A spell that would cause her to fall into a deep, deep sleep. A sleep from which she would awaken 1000 years later.

It's "Sleeping Beauty meets Buck Rogers" in **Sleeping Beauty in the 25th Century**.

Cast Size: 13+ flexible roles with extras possible.

Running Time: 45 minutes.

Royalty: $50.00 per performance.

Appropriate for all audiences.

SNEHURKA A SEDM TRPASLIKU STARE REPUBLIKY

"May the Dwarf be with you in this Czech translation of one our most popular plays!"

A wacky take on the classic fairy tale which will have audiences rolling in the floor with laughter! What happens when you mix an articulate mirror, a conceited Queen, a Prince dressed in purple, seven little people with personality issues, a basket of kumquats and a little Star Wars for good measure?

Snow White and the Seven Dwarves of the Old Republic in Czech!

Cast Size: 12 flexible roles.

Running Time: 45 Minutes.

Royalty: $50.00 per performance.

Appropriate for all audiences.

SNOW WHITE AND THE 47 DWARVES

"May the Dwarf be with you!"

A wacky take on the classic fairy tale which will have audiences rolling in the floor with laughter! What happens when you mix an articulate mirror, a conceited queen, a prince dressed in purple, forty-seven little people with personality issues, a basket of kumquats and throw in a little Star Wars for good measure? **Snow White and the 47 Dwarves!**

Cast Size: 35-70 flexible roles with doubling possible.

Running Time: 90 minutes.

Royalty: $50.00 per performance.

Appropriate for all audiences.

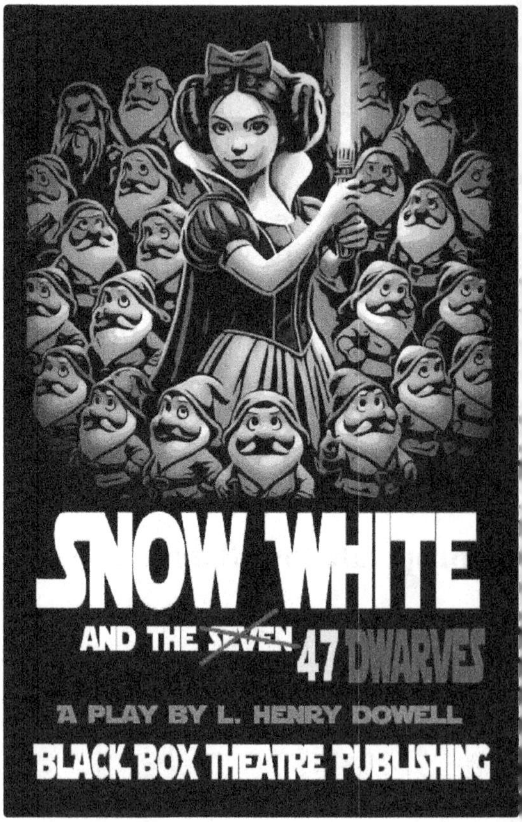

SNOW WHITE AND THE SEVEN DWARVES OF THE OLD REPUBLIC

"May the Dwarf be with you!"

A wacky take on the classic fairy tale which will have audiences rolling in the floor with laughter! What happens when you mix an articulate mirror, a conceited Queen, a Prince dressed in purple, seven little people with personality issues, a basket of kumquats and a little Star Wars for good measure? **Snow White and the Seven Dwarves of the Old Republic!**

This play was first produced in 2007 and since then has gone on to be one of the most produced works for young audiences in the United States.

Cast Size: 12 flexible roles.

Running Time: 45 minutes.

Royalty: $50.00 per performance.

Appropriate for all audiences.

SO, WHO WAS THAT MASKED GUY ANYWAY?

So, Who Was That Masked Guy Anyway? is the story of Ernie, the grandson of the original Masked Cowboy, the legendary lawman who fought for truth, justice and the cowboy way in the old west. Now that Grandpa is getting on in years, he's looking for someone to carry on for him. The only problem? Ernie doesn't know anything about being a cowboy. So, it's off to cowboy school to learn the basics of cowboy-ology. And it's a good thing, because a band of outlaws have captured the good people of Gabby Gulch and the President of the United States, Theodore Roosevelt! Now it's up to Ernie and his friends to save the day...but beware, the poop is sure to hit the fans!

Cast Size: 21+ flexible roles with doubling possible.

Running Time: 90 minutes.

Royalty: $50.00 per performance.

Appropriate for all audiences.

STORY THEATRE

Are you looking for short works that can be performed by young actors for young audiences? Look no further than **Story Theatre**!

It's a collection of short plays written, developed and performed by students at Brownsville Elementary School in Crozet, Virginia under the guidance of Playwright Leslie Tanner.

Cast Size: Varies with each play.

Running Time: Varies with each play.

Royalty: $50.00 per performance.

Appropriate for all audiences.

STUDENT WRITTEN DISASTER

A new comedy by Brent Holland.

Hailey, Dallas and Sam are grouped together in their drama class to write a one act play for their final. With three different authors wanting to drag the play in three different directions we get to see the show transform from a romantic comedy, into fight club and then to a horror show starring El Chupacabra! The characters they are writing come to life on stage and show us each author's view on what should be happening in this teen comedy!

Cast Size: 9 roles with 5M/4F.

Running Time: 40 minutes.

Royalty: $50.00 per performance.

Appropriate for high school audiences.

THE ANNIVERSARY GIFT

"Gifts are important. They're a reflection of one soul's thoughts about another," or so says a TV doctor that Beth listens to. The problem? Her brother-in-law, Marty, gives gifts to Beth's sister, Gladys, that are questionable in Beth's eyes. For example, a spoon with a handle shaped like a squid. Also, a dog collar which is encased in glass. Though Beth is having an intervention to break up her sister's marriage, her sister loves the gifts. When Beth finds out why, she questions Cliff's love for her. Find out what the heck is going on, in this one act comedy about the idiosyncrasies of love.

Cast Size: 4 roles with 2M/2F.

Running Time: 30 minutes.

Royalty: $50.00 per performance.

Appropriate for all audiences.

THE CURE

James Rodgers is a veteran with PTSD from a war to control the only substance found to inhibit the symptoms of the zombie virus decades earlier. He experiences unexplained hallucinations from his time in the war that puts strain on his family and relationships. Meanwhile, the federal government formulates policies cutting medical benefits used to pay for the cure to the remaining carriers of the virus to remain among the living. Rodgers' mother and brother are carriers of the zombie virus, and if the legislation passes, it will lead to their eventual demise. Faced by the nightmares of his past, and the nightmares in his future, Rodgers risks losing everything he loves to prevent his nightmares from becoming a reality.

Cast Size: 30-50 flexible roles possible.

Running Time: 120 minutes.

Royalty: $50.00 per performance.

Appropriate for adult audiences.

THE DRACULA SPECTACULA

Count Dracula is bored. He's pretty much sucked Transylvania dry, and he's looking for a new challenge. So, it's off to New York, New York! Dracula purchases The Carfax Theatre and decides to put on a big, flashy Broadway show...**THE DRACULA SPECTACULA!** Of course, the Theatre just happens to be across the street from Dr. Seward's mental hospital where people have been mysteriously dying since The Count moved in. Just a coincidence? The play features a large cast of zany characters and is equal parts horror story and Broadway show spoof! Dark and funny at the same time!

Cast Size: 30+ flexible roles with doubling possible.

Running Time: 90 minutes.

Royalty: $50.00 per performance.

Appropriate for all audiences.

THE DRACULA SPECTACULA (COMPETITION VERSION)

It's the award-winning competition version of one of our most popular plays! Count Dracula is bored. He's pretty much sucked Transylvania dry, and he's looking for a new challenge. So, it's off to New York, New York! Dracula purchases The Carfax Theatre and decides to put on a big, Broadway show...**THE DRACULA SPECTACULA**! Of course, the Theatre just happens to be across the street from Dr. Seward's mental hospital where people have been mysteriously dying since The Count moved in. Just a coincidence? The play features a large cast of zany characters and is equal parts horror story and Broadway show spoof! Dark and funny at the same time!

Cast Size: 30+ flexible roles with doubling possible.

Running Time: 30 minutes.

Royalty: $50.00 per performance.

Appropriate for all audiences.

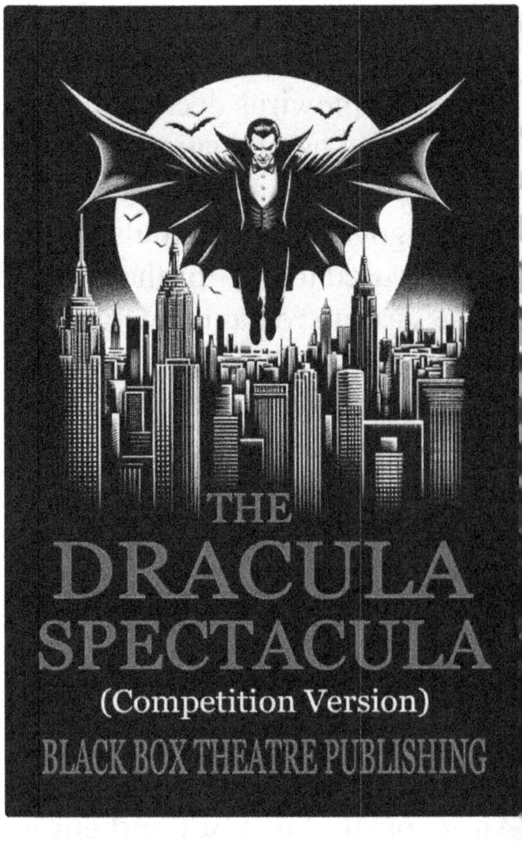

THE FARM OF HENRY KAISER

Set in the 1890's, **The Farm of Henry Kaiser** is about Henry Kaiser, and a prison made by Henry's commitment to his dead wife, Grace, and her dying wish: that her daughter, Gladys, receives the farm upon marriage. Eve, Henry's niece, is blamed by Henry for Grace's death. Henry demands that Eve serve on the farm in the memory of his dead wife. If Eve leaves the farm before Gladys marries, the dying wish of his dead wife will not be fulfilled. But Eve falls in love with Jake, a stranger with a past he cannot escape. The romantic feelings are mutual. They are happy... until Henry finds out. Then, we find out just what lengths Henry will go to in his perverted quest to keep his dead wife's dream alive.

Cast Size: 8 roles with 6M/2F.

Running Time: 75 minutes.

Royalty: $50.00 per performance.

Appropriate for all audiences.

THE FOUR PRESIDENTS

An excellent educational piece based upon a collection of true stories. What does it take to be The President of the United States? What kind of person? **THE FOUR PRESIDENTS** examines these questions as it looks at the lives and characters of four of the most colorful personalities to hold the office: George Washington, Abraham Lincoln, Theodore Roosevelt, and Richard Nixon. Much of the dialogue comes from the presidents' own words.

Cast Size: 10+ roles with doubling possible.

Running Time: 60 minutes.

Royalty: $50.00 per performance.

Appropriate for all audiences.

THE HAIRLESS MONKEYS OF THE STARSHIP BOSTROCK

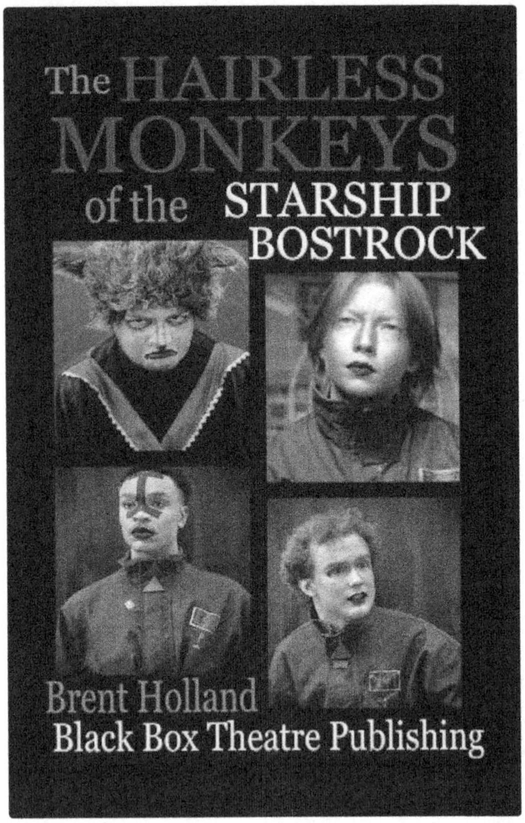

The Crew of the I.F. Starship Bostrock are running harmless, but comedic experiments on the inhabitants of a new planet they have discovered when their ship is attacked and taken over by the evil Damigrians.

Unprepared to defend themselves, the crew of the Bostrock must rely on their human test subjects to help save their ship from being commandeered by the legendary Ezemt Karunch!

Cast Size: 20 roles with 4M/2F/14 Flexible.

Running Time: 90 minutes.

Royalty Rate: $50.00 per performance.

Appropriate for all ages.

THE HEADLESS HORSEMAN OF SLEEPY HOLLOW

The Headless Horseman of Sleepy Hollow is an easy to stage theatrical version of the classic tale by Washington Irving that's scary fun for the entire family. The awkward and superstitious Ichabod Crane has come to the quiet town of Sleepy Hollow to serve as the new School Master.

Until one fateful night, when he comes face to face with the Headless Horseman…or is that Horsemen?

Cast Size: 7+ flexible roles.

Running Time: 45 minutes.

Royalty: $50.00 per performance.

Appropriate for all audiences.

THE INTERVIEW

A one-act play by L. Henry Dowell.

Polish up your resume and make sure your contact list is up to date for this dark, two-person comedy by L. Henry Dowell.

An applicant shows up for an interview only to find out the position is to replace the Grim Reaper themself!

Yikes!

Cast Size: 2 flexible roles.

Running Time: 30 minutes.

Royalty: $35.00 per performance.

Appropriate for all ages.

THE LEGEND OF CHARLIE COPPERHEAD

A one-act play by Zoe and Macy Brown based on a true story. Mild-mannered accountant Charlie Copperhead only wants to get home for Little Pete's birthday party. Little Pete only wants his birthday cake. Heap Big Snake Killer only wants to kill snakes. What will happen when the three of them meet? Find out in The Legend of Charlie Copperhead.

Cast Size: 13 flexible roles.

Running Time: 15 Minutes.

Royalties: $35.00 per performance.

Appropriate for all audiences.

THE LITTLE MERMAID (MORE OR LESS.)

The lights rise on a beautiful sunset. A mermaid is silhouetted against an ocean backdrop. Hauntingly familiar music fills the air. Then...the Lawyer shows up. And the fun begins! **The Little Mermaid (More or Less.)** is the story of a Theatre company attempting to stage a children's version of the Hans Christian Anderson classic. But it looks and sounds an awful lot like a movie of the same name and the Lawyer for a certain "mouse eared company" starts talking lawsuit for copyright infringement. Throw out the costumes! Ditch the music! Change everyone's names! Tartar Sauce! Little M.! The Crab Formerly Known as Sebastian! Everybody ready? Ok...Action!

Cast Size: 30+ flexible M/F roles with doubling possible.

Running Time: 45 minutes.

Royalty: $50.00 per performance.

Appropriate for all audiences.

THE LONG JOHN CAFÉ

It's the end of the world as we know it! Do you know where your icons are? At the edge of the universe sits **The Long John Cafe**. A place where the average guy and the average "Super" guy and can sit and have a cup of coffee and just be themselves or, someone else if that's what they want. The cafe is populated by iconic figures of the 20th Century including cowboys, hippies, super heroes and movie stars. They've come to celebrate the end of the century and the beginning of tomorrow! That is, if they make it through the night. Because the evil Dr. McNastiman has other plans for our heroes. Like their total destruction! Can anyone say...BWAH-HA-HA-HA-HA!?

Cast Size: 17 roles with 9M/8F.

Running Time: 90 minutes.

Royalty: $50.00 per performance.

Appropriate for all audiences.

THE LONG JOHN CAFÉ (COMPETITION VERSION)

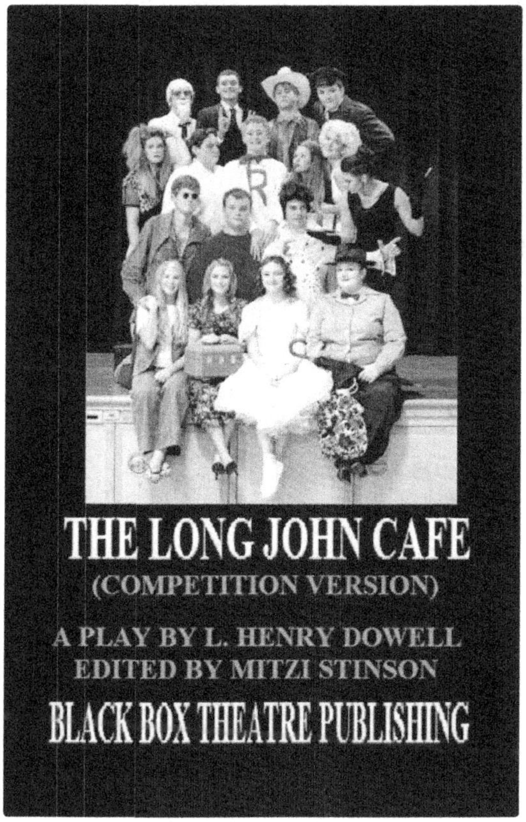

It's the competition version of **THE LONG JOHN CAFÉ**! It's the end of the world as we know it! Do you know where your icons are? At the edge of the universe sits The Long John Cafe. A place where the average guy and the average "Super" guy and can sit and have a cup of coffee and just be themselves or, someone else if that's what they want. The cafe is populated by iconic figures of the 20th Century including cowboys, hippies, super heroes and movie stars. They've come to celebrate the end of the century and the beginning of tomorrow! That is, if they make it through the night. Because the evil Dr. McNasty has other plans for our heroes. Like their total destruction! Can anyone say…BWAH-HA-HA-HA-HA!?

Cast Size: 17+ flexible roles plus extras if desired.

Running Time: 30 minutes.

Royalty: $50.00 per performance.

Appropriate for all audiences.

THE MICE PLAYS

Does anyone ever think about what is important to mice? **The Mice Plays** explores what is important to them.

The Great Mouse Debate, the critical issues of the mouse empire are debated by three candidates for President.

The Fear of All Mice is the story of three mice on a long journey, headed for a wedding, stop and rest. But the rest is interrupted. A terrible foe is reported by one and two of the three mice are convinced their lives are in jeopardy.

In, **One Not So Blind Mouse**, the issue of faith, lack thereof, and action is explored.

Cast Size: 11 roles with 7M/4F.

Running Time: 75 minutes.

Royalty: $50.00 per performance.

Appropriate for all audiences.

THE NEVER BEFORE SEEN PILOT EPISODE OF DIPSY THE DINOSAUR

A whacky full-length comedy from Brent Holland.

Hilarity ensues when four women who walked away from a detention center end up being mistaken for actresses in a children's television show.

Cast Size: 13 roles with 3M/7F and 3 flexible roles.

Running Time: 45 minutes.

Royalty: $50.00 per performance.

Appropriate for all audiences.

THE ODD PRINCESSES

THE ODD PRINCESSES is a parody/mash up that opens with a group of princesses assembled for a card game in the palace of the notoriously messy Snow White.

Late to arrive at the party is the perpetually neat Cinderella who has run away from home after becoming fed up with being treated like a maid by her stepmother.

With nowhere else to turn, the two total opposites decide to move in together! What could go wrong?

Cast Size: 8+ roles with 2M/6F and extras possible.

Running Time: 45 minutes.

Royalty: $50.00 per performance.

Appropriate for all audiences.

THE PIRATE WHO SAVED CHRISTMAS

You think you know the true story of Santa Claus? Think again! Come sail the seven seas with Nicholas the Horrible and his crew of oddball pirates as they seek fame and fortune while engaging in sword clanking battles with weird villains and end up rescuing a group of shipwrecked toys on their way to The Island of Imperfect Playthings! Before it's all over, Nicholas may find the fame he seeks but not as an ill-tempered pirate!!! It's an adventure the entire family can enjoy and perfect for schools looking for a competition play!

Cast Size: 29+ flexible M/F roles with extras possible.

Running Time: 30 Minutes.

Royalty: $50.00 per performance.

Appropriate for all audiences.

THE PRINCESS PLAY COLLECTION

A collection of seven princess plays published by Black Box Theatre Publishing Company. This set includes:

Rapunzel: Escape from Zombie Tower,
The Odd Princesses,
Snow White and the Seven Dwarves of the Old Republic,
The Little Mermaid (More or Less.),
Cinderella and the Quest for the Crystal Pump (Large and small cast versions.),
Sleeping Beauty in the 25th Century, and
Snow White and the 47 Dwarves.

For cast size, running time and royalty information, please see individual listings for each play in this catalog or on our website, www.blackboxtheatrepublishing.com.

THE SLEIGH TEAM

Santa Claus. Frosty. Rudolph. Jack Frost.

This Christmas...if you've got a problem, and if you can find them and you haven't been naughty, then maybe you can hire...

THE SLEIGH TEAM!

The team is hired by lowly clerk, Bob Cratchit to help his boss, the miserly, old Ebenezer Scrooge find a little "Christmas Spirit"!!!

A one-act play that requires minimal scenery.

Cast Size: 6+ flexible roles with extras possible.

Running Time: 60 minutes.

Royalty: $50.00 per performance.

Appropriate for all audiences.

THE TALE OF PETER RABBIT

Based on the book by Beatrix Potter.

The Tale of Peter Rabbit is a short children's play that follows mischievous and disobedient young Peter Rabbit as he gets into, and is chased about, the garden of Mr. McGregor. He escapes and returns home to his mother, who puts him to bed after offering him chamomile-tea.

A perfect play for classroom and competition.

Cast Size: 7 flexible roles.

Running Time: 15 minutes.

Royalty: $35.00 per performance.

Appropriate for all audiences.

THE THROBBIT

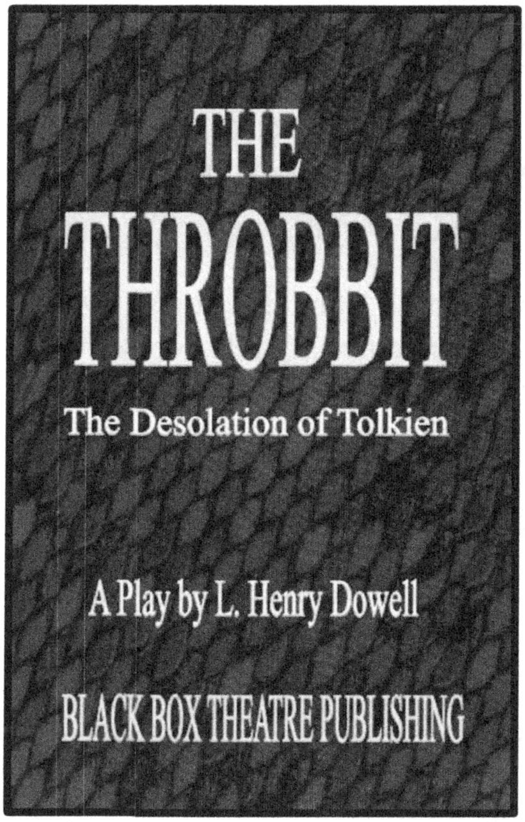

The desolation of Tolkien has begun!

This **MATURE AUDIENCES ONLY** parody of The Hobbit finds Dildo Buggerer and his band of Kiwis journeying through Middle Earth to confront a dragon named Smoo-aww-uggg.

You'll never look at Tolkien the same way again!

Cast Size: 25+ flexible roles with extras possible or doubling if needed.

Running Time: 90 minutes.

Royalty: $50.00 per performance.

Appropriate for mature audiences only.

THE VALUE OF EMPTY BOXES

Veronica, an undiscovered artist in New York City, attends a party with her best friend Barbara, a middle-aged administrative assistant, to meet an unsuccessful blind date. Instead, she meets Bernie, a wealthy roamer and real estate investor and she falls for his eccentric charm. Too soon, Veronica leaves her job to move in with Bernie in San Francisco. Bernie wants to move back to NYC just as Veronica's art career takes off. Veronica must decide whether to move back to New York with Bernie and possibly sacrifice her budding career as well as her independence, or to leave Bernie and stay in San Franscico to follow her dreams. What will she do?

Cast Size: 5 flexible roles.

Running Time: 90 minutes.

Royalty: $50.00 per performance.

Appropriate for mature audiences only.

THE WACKY (YET SERIOUS) MISADVENTURES OF (THE MAN, THE MYTH, THE OUTLAW) ROBIN HOOD AND HIS BAND OF MERRY (YET CAPABLE) MAIDENS IN THE BATTLE FOR (GENDER EQUALITY IN) SHERWOOD FOREST AGAINST THE EVIL (BUT POTENTIALLY MISUNDERSTOOD) SHERIFF OF NOTTINGHAM

It's the wackiest version of Robin Hood that you've ever seen! Robin of Locksley has returned from the crusades to find Maid Marian and the other ladies of Sherwood protesting for equal rights for women. Too serious for your taste? No worries, there's plenty of good-natured fun and gags for the entire family!

Cast Size: 24+ flexible roles with doubling possible.

Running Time: 60 minutes.

Royalty: $50.00 per performance.

Appropriate for all audiences.

THE WACKY (YET SERIOUS) MISADVENTURES OF (THE MAN, THE MYTH, THE OUTLAW) ROBIN HOOD AND HIS BAND OF MERRY (YET CAPABLE) MAIDENS IN THE BATTLE FOR (GENDER EQUALITY IN) SHERWOOD FOREST AGAINST THE EVIL (BUT POTENTIALLY MISUNDERSTOOD) SHERIFF OF NOTTINGHAM (COMPETITION VERSION)

Looking for a competition play for your school? Look no further than this version of our popular Robin Hood parody! Robin of Locksley has returned from the crusades to find Maid Marian and the other ladies of Sherwood protesting for equal rights for women. Too serious? Don't worry, it's good-natured fun and gags for the entire family!

Cast Size: 27+ flexible roles with doubling possible.

Running Time: 30 minutes.

Royalty: $50.00 per performance.

Appropriate for all audiences.

THE WINNING NUMBERS

A play by S. Christopher Boggs.

The buzz around the offices of Dingle, Martin and Associates is "the state lottery is at an all-time high". For employees like Emily and Max, winning the lottery would mean comfort and happiness. For Roberta, it would mean a better education for her twin sons. Louie could finally buy that house he's wanted. Scott could get ahead of the curve. For Stacy and Brewster, it might even mean wedding bells. But when things don't go as planned, and the employees start plotting against each other, the quiet mail room clerk, Alex, starts seeing their true colors.

Cast Size: 10 flexible roles.

Running Time: 180 minutes.

Royalty: $50.00 per performance.

Appropriate for all audiences.

TWISTED TALES

A Narrator begins the production of Twisted Tales only to be bombarded by a new Stage Manager who has been hired to make the play run smoothly. He is met with opposition at every turn, from stagehands not doing their jobs and having to become set pieces, to actors mixing up their cues and eating the props. Meanwhile the actors are humorously acting out three mixed up fairytales: **The 3 Little Riding Hood Pigs, Cinderella and the Beanstalk, Rapunzel and the 7 Dwarfs.** Will the stage manager and actors pull off a successful show? As Cinderella says, "You have to believe in magic!"

Cast Size: 15-40 flexible roles with doubling possible.

Running Time: 45 minutes.

Royalty: $50.00 per performance.

Appropriate for all audiences.

VOLPONE

Based on the Elizabethan classic by Ben Jonson.

Volpone is about a greedy, miserly, old man who lives for excess. He wants everything he sees, and he won't be satisfied until he has it all! But what happens when he takes it too far?

Find out in this great modern text version that'll have audiences rolling in the floor with laughter!

Cast Size: 14 flexible M/F roles with some doubling possible.

Royalty: $50.00 per performance.

Running Time: 120 minutes.

Appropriate for adult audiences.

WANTED: SANTA CLAUS

Santa Claus has been framed! **WANTED: SANTA CLAUS** shows what happens when a group of moguls led by the greedy B.G. Bucks decide to replace Santa Claus with the "KRINGLE 3000", a fully automated, laser guided, multi-faceted miracle of modern technology codenamed: ROBO-SANTA! They will stop at nothing to get rid of jolly old St. Nick, including framing him as purse snatcher, tire thief, and puppy kicker?! But Santa's in no shape to take on his stainless-steel counterpart! Mickey the Elf will get Santa ready for the big showdown! A hilarious play with a serious, yet tender message at its center. **Wanted: Santa Claus** is a great way for the whole family to enjoy the season!

Cast Size: 23+ flexible roles with doubling possible.

Running Time: 90 minutes.

Royalty: $50.00 per performance.

Appropriate for all audiences.

WEIRD ONE-ACTS FOR ODDBALL COLLEGE ACTORS

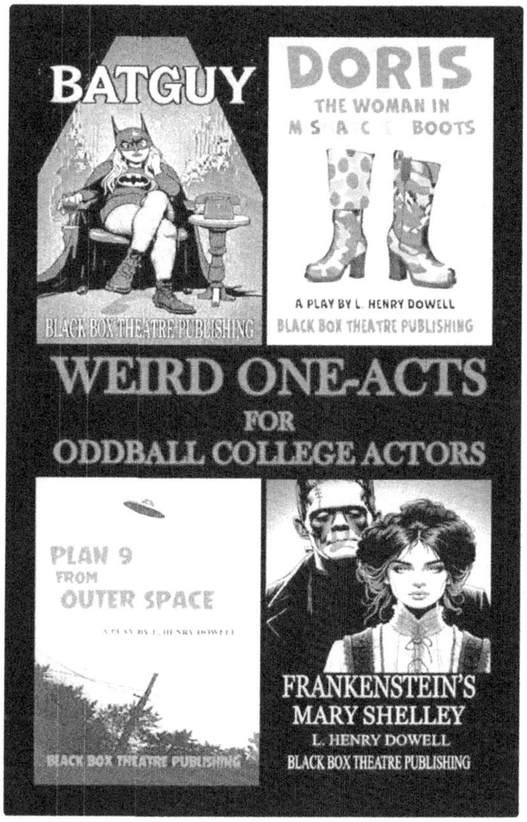

If you have an unusual or quirky sense of humor, then this collection of plays is just what you've been looking for! **Weird One-Acts for Oddball College Actors** is a collection of 14 one-act plays from Author/Playwright, L. Henry Dowell.

BATGUY
CROSSDRESSERS FROM OUTER SPACE
DEAR JOHN
DORIS THE WOMAN IN MISMATCHED BOOTS
ELISHA AND THE BEARS
ELVIS MEETS NIXON
EVEN ADAM
FRANKENSTEIN'S MARY SHELLEY
GODZILLA VS BAMBI
LOSERS
MISS HICKEY'S HICKEY
MY FATHER AND SON
PLAN 9 FROM OUTER SPACE
THE INTERVIEW

For cast size, running time and royalty information, please see individual listings for each play in this catalog or on our website, www.blackboxtheatrepublishing.com.

WINNIE THE POOH

A fun, simple to stage play for all ages based on the works of A. A. Milne.

Winnie the Pooh and all his friends from the Hundred Acre Wood are here in this brand new stage adaptation by L. Henry Dowell, including Piglet, Christopher Robin, Rabbit, Mr. Owl, Eeyore, Kanga, Roo and yes, Tigger too, dressed in a myriad of disguises sure to tickle the funny bone of your audience!

Cast: 17+ flexible roles.

Running Time: 75 minutes.

Royalty: $50.00 per performance.

Appropriate for all audiences.

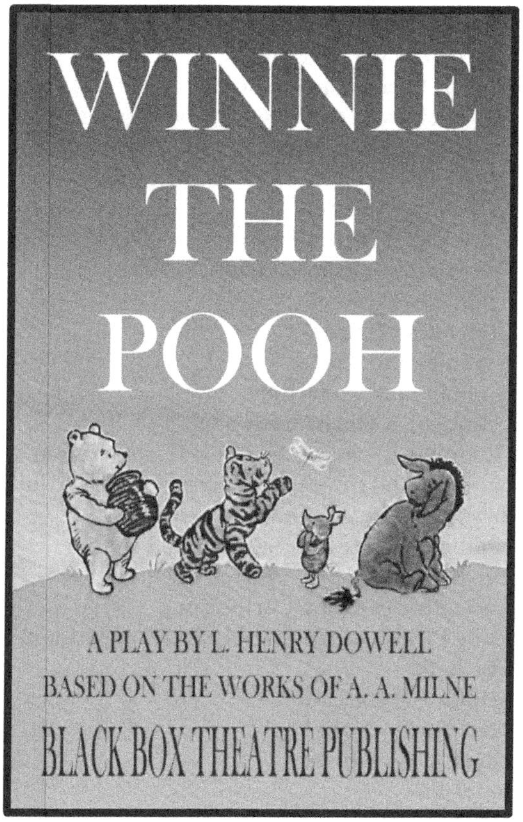

RECOMMENDATIONS

These recommendations are not meant to limit your options. You know best what's appropriate for your group. Most of the plays in this catalog are appropriate for a wide range of audiences.

ELEMENTARY SCHOOL PLAYS

A Squeaky Wheel Gets Oiled
Adventure Play Collection
Batguy (Family Friendly)
Cinderella and the Quest for the Crystal Pump (Large Cast)
Cinderella and the Quest for the Crystal Pump (Small Cast)
Even More Twisted
Fairy Tale Play Collection
Four Famous Kentuckians
Frankenstein Rocks!
Holiday Play Collection
Humbug! A Christmas Carol
Humbug! A Christmas Carol (Competition)
Jacklyn Sparrow and the Lady Pirates of the Caribbean
Jemima Boone: Daughter of the Frontier
Jurassic Pork
Lady Pirates of the Caribbean
Lady Pirates of the Caribbean (Competition)
Rapunzel: Escape from Zombie Tower
Sleeping Beauty in the 25th Century
Snerhuka A Sedm Trpasliku Stare Republiky
Snow White and the 47 Dwarves
Snow White and the Seven Dwarves of the Old Republic
So, Who Was That Masked Guy Anyway?
Story Theatre
The Dracula Spectacula
The Dracula Spectacula (Competition)
The Four Presidents
The Headless Horseman of Sleepy Hollow
The Legend of Charlie Copperhead
The Little Mermaid (More or Less.)
The Odd Princesses
The Pirate Who Saved Christmas
The Princess Play Collection
The Sleigh Team
The Tale of Peter Rabbit
The Wacky Misadventures of Robin Hood
The Wacky Misadventures of Robin Hood (Competition)
Twisted Tales
Wanted: Santa Claus
Winnie the Pooh

MIDDLE SCHOOL PLAYS

A Midsummer Night's Dream
A Squeaky Wheel Gets Oiled
Adventure Play Collection
Batguy (Family Friendly)
Cinderella and the Quest for the Crystal Pump (Large Cast)
Cinderella and the Quest for the Crystal Pump (Small Cast)
Dracula vs Santa Claus
Doris: The Woman in Mismatched Boots
Even More Twisted
Fairy Tale Play Collection
Four Famous Kentuckians
Frankenstein Rocks!
Godzilla vs Bambi
Hercules and Chuck
Holiday Play Collection
Humbug! A Christmas Carol
Humbug! A Christmas Carol (Competition)
Jacklyn Sparrow and the Lady Pirates of the Caribbean
Jason and the Argonauts
Jemima Boone: Daughter of the Frontier
Jurassic Pork
Lady Pirates of the Caribbean
Lady Pirates of the Caribbean (Competition)
Macbeth
Middle School Live
Miss Hickey's Hickey
Night of the Muses
Peter Pan
Peter Pan (Competition)
Popeye
Rapunzel: Escape from Zombie Tower
Shorespeare (Large Cast)
Shorespeare (Small Cast)
Sleeping Beauty in the 25th Century
Snerhuka A Sedm Trpasliku Stare Republiky
Snow White and the 47 Dwarves
Snow White and the Seven Dwarves of the Old Republic
So, Who Was That Masked Guy Anyway?
Story Theatre
Student Written Disaster
The Dracula Spectacula
The Dracula Spectacula (Competition)
The Four Presidents
The Headless Horseman of Sleepy Hollow
The Legend of Charlie Copperhead
The Little Mermaid (More or Less.)
The Long John Café
The Long John Café (Competition)
The Odd Princesses
The Pirate Who Saved Christmas
The Princess Play Collection
The Sleigh Team
The Wacky Misadventures of Robin Hood
The Wacky Misadventures of Robin Hood (Competition)
Twisted Tales
Wanted: Santa Claus
Winnie the Pooh

HIGH SCHOOL PLAYS

A Midsummer Night's Dream
Abraham Lincoln: The Great8 Emancipator
Adventure Play Collection
Based On The...
Batguy (Family Friendly)
Cinderella and the Quest for the Crystal Pump (Large Cast)
Cinderella and the Quest for the Crystal Pump (Small Cast)
Curious Tales for Christmas
Dear John: An Ode to the Potty
Doris: The Woman in Mismatched Boots
Dracula vs Santa Claus
Elisha and the Bears
Elvis Meets Nixon
Even Adam
Even More Twisted
Exits and Entrances
Fairy Tale Play Collection
Finger Lickin' Good! The Story of Colonel Sanders
Four Famous Kentuckians
Frankenstein Rocks!
Frankenstein's Mary Shelley
Frontier Surgeon: The Story of Dr. Ephraim McDowell
Godzilla vs Bambi
Hercules and Chuck
High School Live
Holiday Play Collection
Humbug! A Christmas Carol
Humbug! A Christmas Carol (Competition)
Jacklyn Sparrow and the Lady Pirates of the Caribbean
Jason and the Argonauts
Jemima Boone: Daughter of the Frontier
Jurassic Pork
Lady Pirates of the Caribbean
Lady Pirates of the Caribbean (Competition)
Losers
Macbeth
Masked Men
Miss Hickey's Hickey
My Father and Son
Night of the Muses
Peter Pan
Peter Pan (Competition)
Plan 9 from Outer Space
Popeye
Pulling Leather (Family Friendly)
Pursued by a Runaway Train
Rapunzel: Escape from Zombie Tower
Roses are Red: A 1930's Radio Drama
Seven Dreams of Falling
Shorespeare (Large Cast)
Shorespeare (Small Cast)
Sleeping Beauty in the 25th Century
Snerhuka A Sedm Trpasliku Stare Republiky
Snow White and the 47 Dwarves
Snow White and the Seven Dwarves of the Old Republic
So, Who Was That Masked Guy Anyway?
Student Written Disaster
The Cure
The Dracula Spectacula
The Dracula Spectacula (Competition)
The Farm of Henry Kaiser
The Four Presidents
The Hairless Monkeys of the Starship Bostrock
The Headless Horseman of Sleepy Hollow
The Interview
The Little Mermaid (More or Less.)
The Long John Café
The Long John Café (Competition)
The Mice Plays
The Never Before Seen Pilot Episode of Dipsy the Dinosaur
The Odd Princesses
The Pirate Who Saved Christmas
The Princess Play Collection
The Sleigh Team
The Wacky Misadventures of Robin Hood
The Wacky Misadventures of Robin Hood (Competition)
The Winning Numbers
Twisted Tales
Volpone
Wanted: Santa Claus
Winnie the Pooh

COLLEGE AND ADULT THEMED PLAYS

A Midsummer Night's Dream
A Persecution Story
Based On The...
Batguy (Mature)
Crossdressers From Outer Space
Curious Tales for Christmas
Dear John: An Ode to the Potty
Divanalysis
Doris: The Woman in Mismatched Boots
Dracula vs Santa Claus
Elisha and the Bears
Elvis Meets Nixon
Even Adam
Exits and Entrances
Finger Lickin' Good! The Story of Colonel Sanders
Four Famous Kentuckians
Frankenstein Rocks!
Frankenstein's Mary Shelley
Frontier Surgeon: The Story of Dr. Ephraim McDowell
Godzilla vs Bambi
Hercules and Chuck
Humbug! A Christmas Carol
Humbug! A Christmas Carol (Competition)
Humbug! A One Man Christmas Carol
Infectious
Jacklyn Sparrow and the Lady Pirates of the Caribbean
Jemima Boone: Daughter of the Frontier
Lady Pirates of the Caribbean
Legends and Bridge
Losers

Macbeth
Masked Men
My Father and Son
Peter Pan
Plan 9 from Outer Space
Popeye
Pulling Leather (Family Friendly)
Pulling Leather (Mature)
Pursued by a Runaway Train
Rapunzel: Escape from Zombie Tower
Roses are Red: A 1930's Radio Drama
Second Year Itch
Seven Dreams of Falling
Sleeping Beauty in the 25th Century
Snerhuka A Sedm Trpasliku Stare Republiky
Snow White and the 47 Dwarves
Snow White and the Seven Dwarves of the Old Republic
So, Who Was That Masked Guy Anyway?
The Anniversary Gift
The Cure
The Dracula Spectacula
The Farm of Henry Kaiser
The Four Presidents
The Headless Horseman of Sleepy Hollow
The Interview
The Little Mermaid (More or Less.)
The Long John Café
The Mice Plays
The Odd Princesses
The Pirate Who Save Christmas
The Sleigh Team
The Throbbit
The Value of Empty Boxes
The Wacky Adventure of Robin Hood
The Winning Numbers
Volpone
Wanted: Santa Claus
Weird One-Acts for Oddball College Actors
Winnie the Pooh

COMPETITION PLAYS

Batguy (Family Friendly)
Dear John: An Ode to the Potty
Doris: The Woman in Mismatched Boots
Eli
Elvis Meets Nixon
Even Adam
Frankenstein Rocks!
Frankenstein's Mary Shelley
Godzilla vs Bambi
Hercules and Chuck
High School Live
Humbug! A Christmas Carol (Competition)
Jason and the Argonauts
Jurassic Pork
Lady Pirates of the Caribbean (Competition)
Middle School Live
Miss Hickey's Hickey
Night of the Muses
Peter Pan (Competition)
Snow White and the Seven Dwarves of the Old Republic
The Dracula Spectacula (Competition)
The Four Presidents
The Headless Horseman of Sleepy Hollow
The Interview
The Little Mermaid (More or Less.)
The Long John Café (Competition)
The Mice Plays
The Odd Princesses
The Pirate Who Saved Christmas
The Sleigh Team
The Wacky Misadventures of Robin Hood (Competition)

HOLIDAY PLAYS

Curious Tales for Christmas
Dracula vs Santa Claus
Frankenstein Rocks!
Frankenstein's Mary Shelley
Holiday Play Collection
Humbug! A Christmas Carol
Humbug! A Christmas Carol (Competition)
Humbug! A One Man Christmas Carol
Plan 9 from Outer Space
Rapunzel: Escape from Zombie Tower
The Dracula Spectacula
The Dracula Spectacula (Competition)
The Four Presidents
The Headless Horseman of Sleepy Hollow
The Interview
The Pirate Who Saved Christmas
The Sleigh Team
Wanted: Santa Claus

1 - 3 PERSON PLAYS

Abraham Lincoln: The Great Emancipator
Based On The...
Curious Tales for Christmas
Divanalysis
Elvis Meets Nixon
Even Adam
Finger Lickin' Good! The Story of Colonel Sanders
Four Famous Kentuckians
Frontier Surgeon: The Story of Dr. Ephraim McDowell
Jemima Boone: Daughter of the Frontier
Losers
Masked Men
My Father and Son
The Interview